I0042584

THE STATE OF FOOD INSECURITY IN MSUNDUZI MUNICIPALITY, SOUTH AFRICA

MARY CAESAR, JONATHAN CRUSH
AND TREVOR HILL

SERIES EDITOR: PROF. JONATHAN CRUSH

Acknowledgements

The research for this project was funded by the Canadian International Development Agency (CIDA) under the UPCD Tier One Program. We would like to thank the following who assisted with the project in various ways: Wade Pendleton, Bronwen Dachs, Christa Schier, Bruce Frayne and Robert Fincham.

AFSUN

© AFSUN 2013

Published by the African Food Security Urban Network (AFSUN)
African Centre for Cities, University of Cape Town, Private Bag X3
Rondebosch 7701, South Africa; and
Southern African Research Centre, Queen's University,
152 Albert Street, Kingston, ON K7L 3N6, Canada
www.afsun.org

First published 2013

ISBN 978-1-920597-07-8

Cover photograph by Ian Carbutt, *The Witness*

Production by Bronwen Dachs Müller, Cape Town

AUTHORS

Mary Caesar is a Researcher at the Southern African Research Centre, Queen's University.

Jonathan Crush is Director of the African Food Security Urban Network.

Trevor Hill is Professor in the Department of Geography, University of KwaZulu-Natal.

Previous Publications in the AFSUN Series

CONTENTS

TABLES

FIGURES

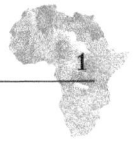

1. INTRODUCTION

The Msunduzi Municipality (hereafter "Msunduzi") is the provincial capital of the South African province of KwaZulu-Natal (Figure 1). The restructuring of municipal boundaries in 2000 created the newly-expanded capital city by combining Edendale, one of the largest urban townships in the province, and Pietermaritzburg, the previous capital.[1] The 2011 Census recorded over 600,000 people in 164,000 households within the Msunduzi municipal boundaries.[2] Like all South African cities, Msunduzi shows signs of the apartheid legacy, including "uneven development between city and suburbs, the spatial allocation of land – which still runs along strongly racial lines – and the serious underdevelopment in traditionally 'black' townships."[3] Nearly 20 years after the country's first democratic elections, high levels of unemployment and problems in delivery of basic services indicate that improvement in the lives of the city's urban poor remains a major challenge. The dimensions of this challenge have been explored in relation to issues including housing, water, electricity, sanitation and health.[4] However, food security has been given insufficient attention in research on poverty and livelihoods in Msunduzi, and KwaZulu-Natal more generally, and the research that does exist focuses on rural food security.[5]

The Integrated Development Plan (IDP) for 2011-2016 of the Msunduzi Municipality has nothing substantial to say about food security, other than repeating President Jacob Zuma's 2011 State of the Nation call for a rural development strategy linked to land reform and food security.[6] The 2010 Draft Strategic Environmental Assessment for Msunduzi does contain several references to food security, however.[7] For example, the report notes that the municipality should "take steps to eradicate hunger, malnutrition and food insecurity by 2015."[8] To achieve this objective, the report proposes (a) an urban greening programme using indigenous trees and, where appropriate, fruit trees, to enhance food security; and (b) ensuring that most of the daily food needs of Msunduzi are sustainably grown, processed and packaged in rural and urban agricultural schemes in the city and surrounding rural areas.[9] The report contains no information or analysis on the extent and determinants of food insecurity in Msunduzi. Rather than being based on substantive information about the state of food security, the recommendations are generic solutions that reflect broader, and problematic, thinking about urban food security in South Africa and elsewhere.[10]

In order to better understand the nature and determinants of urban food insecurity in Southern Africa, the AFSUN baseline food security survey was implemented in 2008 and 2009 in 11 SADC cities, including Msunduzi.[11] The Msunduzi questionnaire was administered to a sample of 556 households in the poorer parts of the city (Figure 2). The selected areas represent different types of neighbourhood including new and old townships, informal settlements and peri-urban areas with traditional housing. Households were randomly selected for interview within each area. Based on the results of the survey, this report does three things. First, it provides the first detailed empirical analysis of the prevalence and determinants of food insecurity at the household level in Msunduzi. The data provides a substantive basis on which to think about the complex policy challenges of mitigating food insecurity in the city. Second, the report examines the issue of which households are most vulnerable to food insecurity and which should therefore be targeted in any strategy to alleviate food insecurity. And third, it examines the food sourcing and livelihood strategies deployed by households and shows that current proposals for eliminating food insecurity in the city need to be reconsidered.

FIGURE 1: Location of Msunduzi

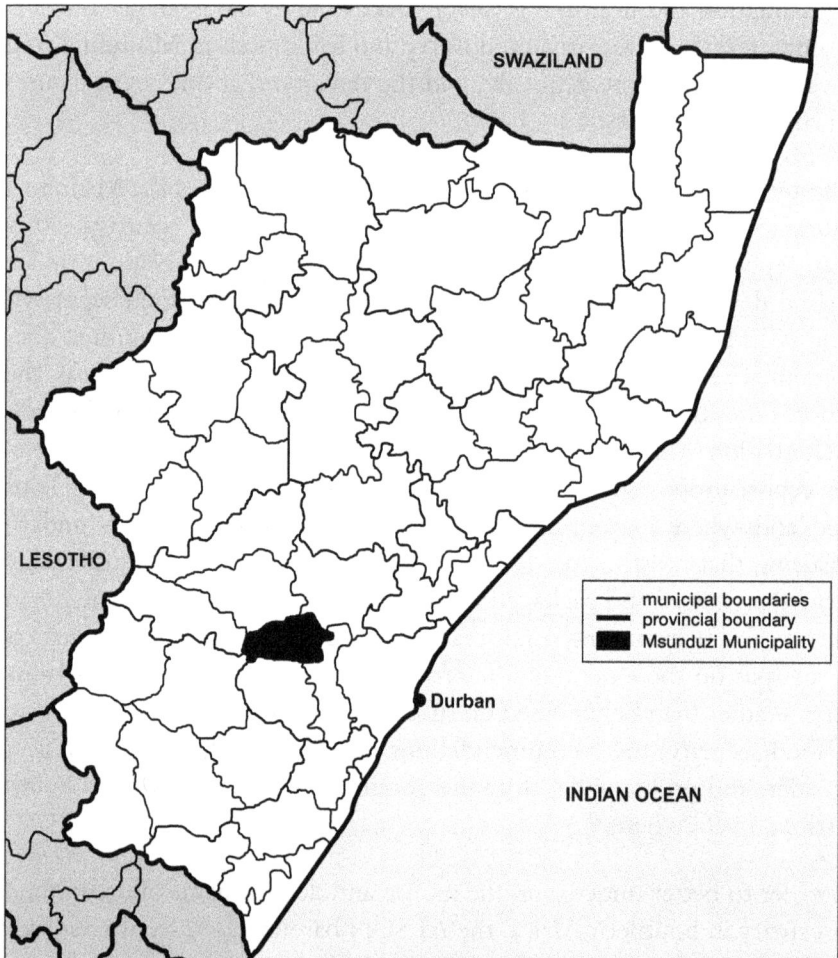

FIGURE 2: Msunduzi Municipality

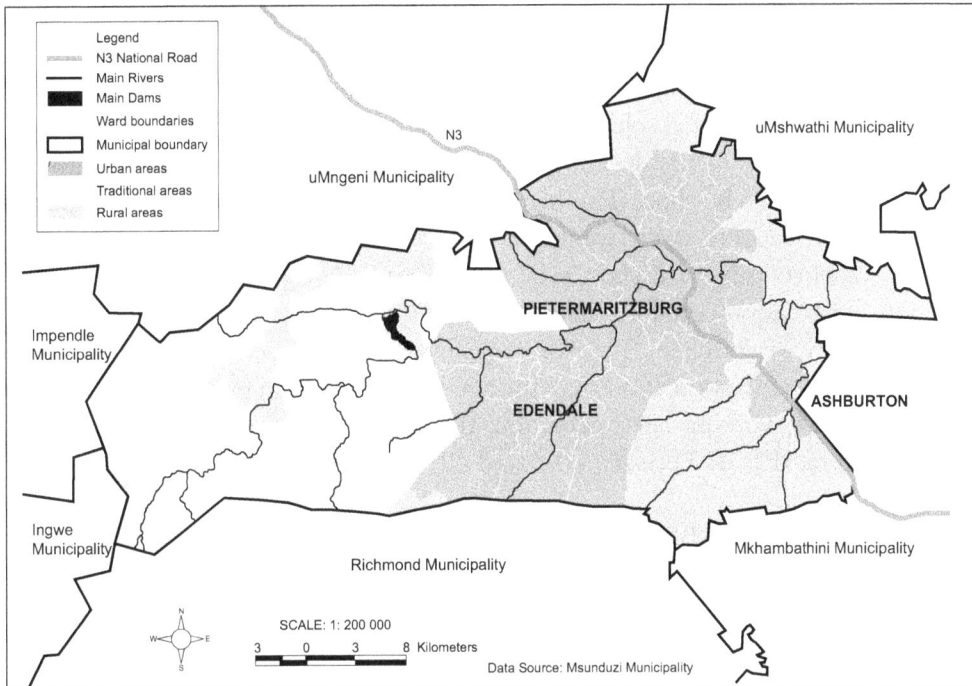

2. DEMOGRAPHIC PROFILE

The South African Censuses of 1996, 2001 and 2011 provide basic data to construct an overall demographic profile of the Msunduzi population and to show how the profile has changed over the past 15 years.[12] The data also provides a point of comparison with the survey sample of Msunduzi households in the AFSUN survey. The total population of Msunduzi increased from 521,000 in 1996 to 617,000 in 2011 (an increase of nearly 20%). The black African population of the city increased by 120,000, while both the white and Indian/Asian population have been in steady decline. Proportionally, the black African population increased from 73% in 1996 to 81% in 2011.[13]

TABLE 1: Population of Msunduzi, 1996–2011						
	1996		2001		2011	
	No.	%	No.	%	No.	%
Black African	381,099	73.0	424,654	76.9	501,506	81.3
Indian/Asian	68,113	13.1	64,821	11.7	60,591	9.8
White	56,154	10.8	44,954	8.1	36,860	6.0
Coloured	16,096	3.1	18,408	3.3	17,758	2.9
Total	521,462	100.0	552,837	100.0	616,715	100.0
Source: Statistics South Africa						

The population of Msunduzi is primarily young, with around half of the residents under 30 years of age and nearly 40% under 20 years of age.[14] What is interesting about this profile, however, is the apparent drop in the proportion of children and youth from 40% to 37% between 2001 and 2011. The absolute number in the 10–19 age group actually fell over the course of the decade, possibly because some are being sent to other areas for schooling. The biggest absolute increase was in the number of individuals in their twenties and thirties, despite the fact that this is the cohort with the highest HIV prevalence and AIDS mortality rates. One explanation could be that, as an industrial town, Msunduzi is attracting more workseekers. The other age cohort increase between 2001 and 2011 was in the population over the age of 60. Reflecting the relative increase in the working-age population, the dependency ratio for Msunduzi fell from 51 to 46 between 2001 and 2011.

The survey sample was even more youthful than the general population with almost 70% of household members under the age of 30 (Figure 3). Thirty-four percent of the total population were under the age of 15 and 12% were under the age of 5. In other words, households in the poorer parts of the city have significantly higher numbers of people under 30 and children under 5. The high number of children in the sample has particular implications for food security since they are especially prone to the worst effects of undernutrition, including wasting and stunting.[15] This also means that large numbers of household members are not generating income and are dependent for food on the household head. As a group, they are also highly vulnerable to the impact of HIV and AIDS on the household.[16]

TABLE 2: Age Distribution of Msunduzi Population, 2001–2011				
	2001		2011	
	No.	%	No.	%
0–9	103,950	19	111,330	18
10–19	118,654	21	115,319	19
20–29	112,532	20	136,174	22
30–39	81,688	15	94,711	15
40–49	58,670	11	65,694	11
50–59	37,595	7	46,634	7
60–69	22,797	4	28,962	5
70+	16,889	3	19,722	3
Total	552,837	100	618,536	100
Source: Statistics South Africa				

FIGURE 3: Age Distribution of Survey Household Members

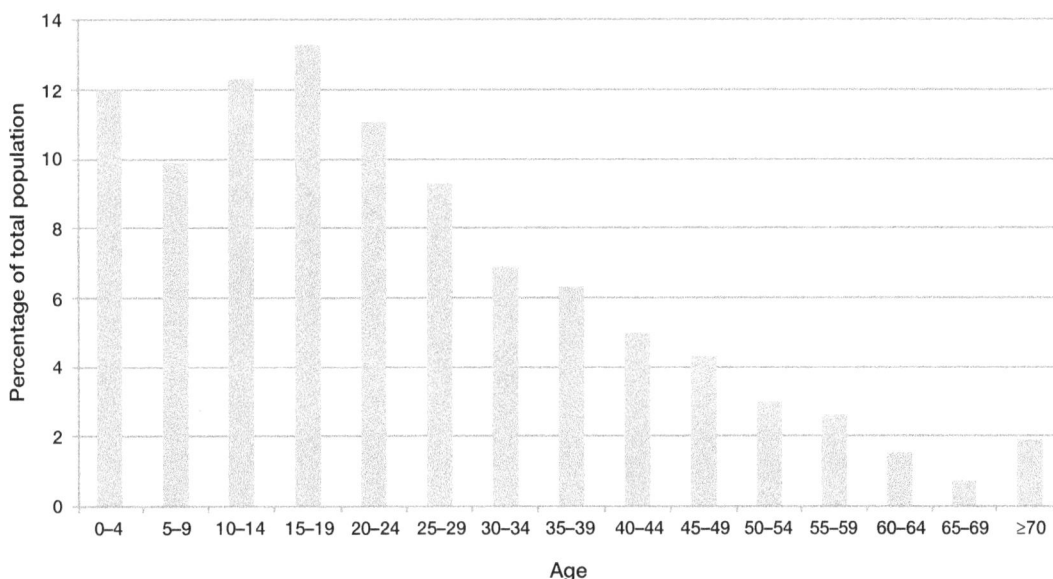

The majority of household heads in the survey were of working age. Some 11% were in their twenties, 24% were in their thirties and 25% were in their forties (Figure 4). A small number of household heads (14% of the total) were 60 years old and over and therefore of pensionable and/or retirement age under South African welfare laws and employment regulations. In general, this age cohort has become increasingly important as primary caregivers of children as younger, economically-active adults become ill or die of AIDS-related diseases.[17]

The national Department of Health estimates that more than 5 million South Africans were HIV-positive in 2006 and about 400,000 individuals died of AIDS-related illness in 2007. KwaZulu-Natal, the most populous province, has the highest rates of HIV and AIDS in the country. Msunduzi was one of the first municipalities in South Africa to develop an HIV and AIDS strategy, well before the national and provincial local government strategies were rolled out in 2006–2007.[18] At that time (in 2001), 36% of attendees at ante-natal clinics were HIV-positive and the number of HIV-related infections was estimated at 88,000 (or 18% of the total population). The elderly are not the only ones taking on care responsibilities. Typical of a community experiencing the effects of AIDS, Msunduzi also has young household heads. In the survey, 14 heads were younger than 24 years of age, with the youngest being 19. At the same time, the survey identified no child-headed households, which may be more of a rural phenomenon.

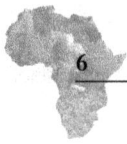

FIGURE 4: Age Distribution of Survey Household Heads

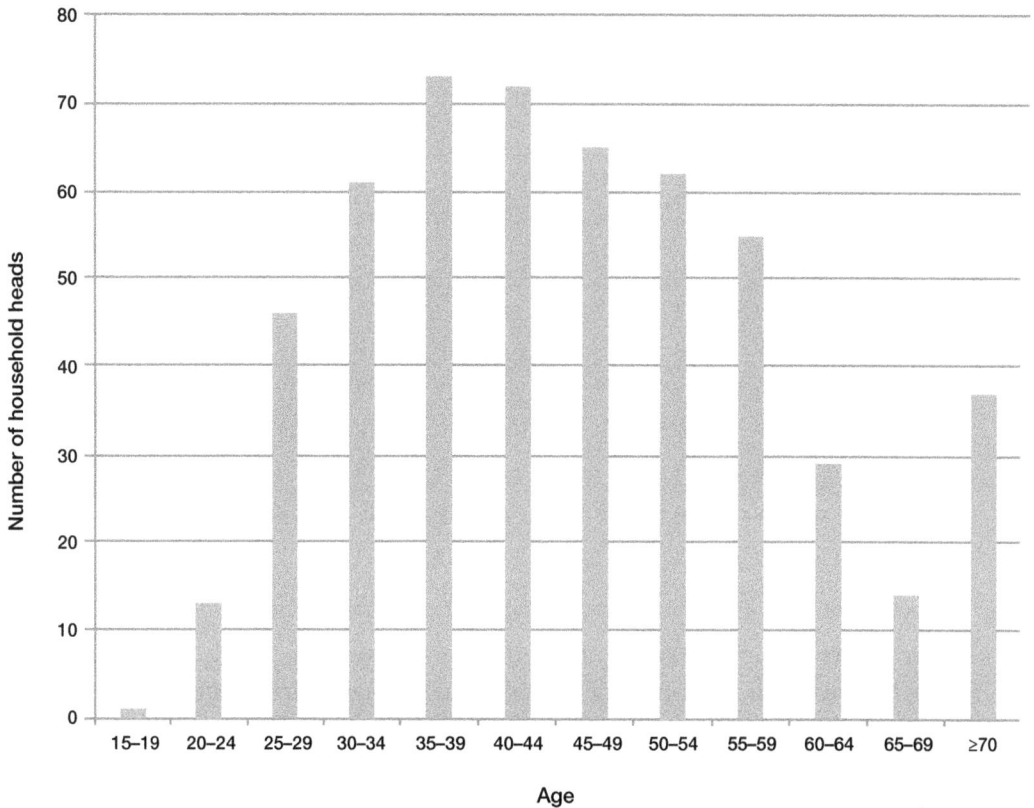

The number of households in Msunduzi grew from 117,149 in 1996 to 130,292 in 2001 to 163,993 in 2011. At the same time, there was a decline in average household size from 4.5 in 1996 to 4.1 in 2001 to 3.6 in 2011.[19] This is certainly not unique to Msunduzi or even KwaZulu-Natal. One study, undertaken prior to the 2011 Census, found evidence of "rapidly shrinking size" of households throughout South Africa.[20] The average household size in the survey was certainly much larger than the Censuses of both 2001 and 2011. An average of 5.2 (median of 5.0) suggests that poorer households may not be "unbundling" at the same rate as in the area as a whole. However, as many as 63% of households had between one and five members. The larger households tended to be extended family units while most of the smaller households were female or male-centred.[21]

The number of female-centred households in Msunduzi has been steadily increasing over the past decade and a half from 41,000 in 1996 to 58,000 in 2001 to 74,000 in 2011.[22] The proportion of female-centred households increased from 35% to 45% over the same period. In the AFSUN survey sample, 53% of the households were female-centred, suggesting that they are disproportionately represented in the poorer areas of the city

(Table 3). There were far fewer nuclear households (22% of the total) and extended and male-centred households (13% and 12% respectively).

TABLE 3: Structure of Surveyed Households		
Type of household	No.	%
Female-centred	296	53.2
Male-centred	66	11.9
Nuclear	120	21.6
Extended	74	13.3
Total	556	100.0

Nineteen percent of the total survey population were household heads (Table 4). Again reflecting the youthfulness of the sample, 41% were sons/daughters of the head and 17% were grandchildren. Less than 1% were grandparents of the head and less than 2% were adopted/orphans/foster children. The proportion of other non-relatives was also very small (at less than 2%). Slightly more were brothers or sisters of the head (5%) and extended family members (7%). In other words, households tend to be made up of direct blood relatives of the head with very few distant relatives and non-relatives in residence. The small numbers of child-headed households as well as adopted, orphaned and foster children suggest that so-called "AIDS orphans" tend to be cared for by family rather than non-relatives.

TABLE 4: Relationship of Household Members to Household Head		
	No.	%
Household heads	556	19.4
Spouses/partners	194	6.8
Sons/daughters	1,170	40.8
Grandchildren	481	16.8
Brothers/sisters	156	5.4
Grandparents	4	0.1
Sons/daughters-in-law	23	0.8
Other relatives	193	6.7
Adopted/orphans/foster children	35	1.2
Non-relatives	38	1.3
Total	2,871	100.0

The marital status of household members in the surveyed households was similar to that of the population as a whole in both 2001 and 2011, with around one quarter being married and nearly 70% unmarried.[23] Rates of widowhood and divorce/separation were also roughly equivalent. In gen-

eral, despite the impact of HIV and AIDS, the number of widowed in the total population dropped from 24,000 to 21,000 between 2001 and 2011.

TABLE 5: Marital Status of Msunduzi Population			
	Census 2001 (%)	Census 2011 (%)	AFSUN Survey (%)
Married	26.1	26.4	25.0*
Unmarried	68.0	68.6	69.9
Widowed	4.4	3.5	3.9
Divorced/separated	1.5	1.5	1.3
*Includes married and living together/co-habiting			

The apartheid legacy can be glimpsed in the educational achievements (or lack thereof) in the adult population of Msunduzi and, specifically, in the survey sample of adults in the poor neighbourhoods of the city (Table 6). The fall in the overall numbers with primary education or less (from 32% in 2001 to 20% in 2011), and increase in those with secondary education (from 59% to 67%), is testimony to the expansion of basic education after the end of apartheid. However, the AFSUN survey (in late 2008) found similar levels of no schooling, primary education and some secondary education as in 2001 and much lower levels of completed secondary education and post-secondary education than in either 2001 or 2011.

TABLE 6: Level of Education of Adult Population (20+)			
	Census 2001	Census 2011	AFSUN survey
No schooling	10.7	5.5	6.9
Some primary	15.2	10.6	18.3
Complete primary	6.1	3.7	5.7
Some secondary	34.9	33.3	43.8
Complete secondary	24.1	34.1	19.9
Higher	9.0	12.8	1.7

The past decade in Msunduzi has seen an increase in the proportion of households living in formal dwellings (from 69% in 2001 to 75% in 2011) and a decline in the number and proportion of informal dwellings (from 12% in 2001 to 8% in 2011) (Table 7).[24] This places Msunduzi in a rather different position from many other cities in South Africa and the Southern African region where informal settlements are growing rapidly. A housing summit in Msunduzi in mid-2012 reported, however, that the pace of formal housing delivery was causing immense frustration in the poorer areas of the city and that new informal structures were "mushrooming" as a result.[25] What cannot be assumed is that households in Msunduzi are necessarily better off because they do not live in the large informal settlements that characterize other cities. Most of the formal housing occupied

by households in this survey was basic, low-cost housing in low-income areas.[26] The "other" category (comprising 7% of the sample) includes households living in backyards, rented rooms, caravans and hostels.

TABLE 7: Housing in Msunduzi			
	Census 2001 (%)	Census 2011 (%)	AFSUN survey (%)
Formal housing	69.3	74.9	56.8
Informal housing	12.5	8.4	19.5
Traditional/rural	18.2	16.7	16.8
Other			7.0
Total	100.0	100.0	100.0

3. Socio-Economic Profile

The economic base of Msunduzi is relatively diverse with services and manufacturing especially prominent. A recent International Labour Organization (ILO) review of the local economy notes that the manufacturing sector (which includes aluminium products, automotive components, footwear and furniture) makes up just over a third of total turnover, followed by wholesale and retail trade (24%) and business services. In terms of employment generation, the service sector has the largest workforce (27%), followed by manufacturing and wholesale/retail (both at 15%).[27] The report observes that five to 10 years ago, Msunduzi was in serious economic decline with no new outside investment and rising unemployment and poverty. The area's shoe manufacturing industry had collapsed due to cheap imports, shedding 4,500 jobs between 1990 and 2003.[28] To address the challenge, the local government embarked on an aggressive campaign to market the city and attract investment. According to the ILO, the results of this pro-growth strategy were "startling" with several thousand new jobs being created and declining unemployment.[29] Unemployment levels in the city as a whole were at 40% in 1996 and 48% in 2001 but had fallen to 33% in 2011.[30]

Has this economic "mini-boom" had a positive impact on the urban poor? The survey found that only 21% of the adult population were in full-time employment, with another 18% working part-time or casually (Table 8). This left 61% who were either unemployed and looking for work (35%) or unemployed and not looking for work (26%). Since the Census applies a strict definition of unemployment (unemployed and looking), the unemployment rate in the surveyed households is similar to that for the city as a whole (33% in 2011). The unemployment rate in the survey sample was higher for women than men (38% versus 32%). The other significant, and related, gender difference was in the relative proportions in full-time employment: 28% of male household members versus only 15% of females.

TABLE 8: Employment Status of Adult Household Members			
	No.	Female	Male
Working full-time	20.8	14.7	28.0
Working part-time/casual	17.6	16.9	18.3
Unemployed – looking for work	35.2	38.0	31.9
Unemployed – not looking for work	26.4	30.4	21.8
Total	1,517	821	696

Average annual household income in Msunduzi was R50,178 in 2001 and R108,926 in 2011, another indicator of improvement in the local economy over the past decade.[31] The average household income for the surveyed households was only R24,420, half the city average in 2001 and only a quarter of the average in 2011. Why are these households significantly worse off in terms of earnings than the average in the city? The answer lies in the fact that the majority of the jobs performed by household members are low-paying and menial in nature and households do not have many alternative income streams. As a group, the surveyed households had three main sources of income: social grants, wage employment and part-time work (Table 9). Social grants (in the form of child grants and pensions) were an income source for two thirds of the households. A total of 38% of households obtained some income through wage work and 32% earned income from casual labour. One significant difference between female-centred households and other households lies in the proportion receiving income from wage work (28% versus 48%). This is consistent with the observation above that men find it easier to get wage employment than women.

The average income from wage work in the surveyed households was R32,000 per annum and R14,000 per annum from casual work. Average income from casual work was significantly higher than average social grant income (at R9,600 per annum). All other potential sources of income were relatively insignificant: only 8% of households earned income from informal sector activity and less than 1% earned anything from the sale of agricultural produce. What this suggests is that access to employment is the critical determinant of household income. And, in turn, this means that female-centred households are at a significant disadvantage. However, even amongst those in wage employment, there is a significant gender difference. Those female-centred households with a wage worker, for example, earn an average of R21,976 per annum compared with an average of R38,148 per annum by other households. Similarly with casual work, where the figures are R10,464 (female-centred households) and R17,268 (other households). The gender differences are also apparent in the income tercile data where female-centred households are dispropor-tionately represented in the lowest income tercile and other households in the upper income tercile (Figure 5). Households unable to place a mem-ber in wage employment therefore face a considerable struggle to make ends meet through a combination of low-paying casual work, social grant income and, for a few, scraping by in the informal economy.

TABLE 9: Sources of Household Income

	Female-centred households	Other households	% of total households	Average annual income from source
Main sources				
Social grants	68.2	60.9	65.5	R9,636
Wage work	28.4	48.1	38.1	R31,932
Casual work	29.0	34.2	32.2	R13,788
Other sources				
Informal economy	12.5	11.5	8.4	R13,488
Rentals	3.4	2.7	2.9	R3,060
Remittances	3.0	2.3	2.7	R5,880
Gifts	1.7	0.4	1.1	R19,200
Sale of farm produce	0.3	0.8	0.5	R7,800
Formal business	0.0	0.4	0.1	R120,000

FIGURE 5: Income Terciles of Female-Centred and Other Households

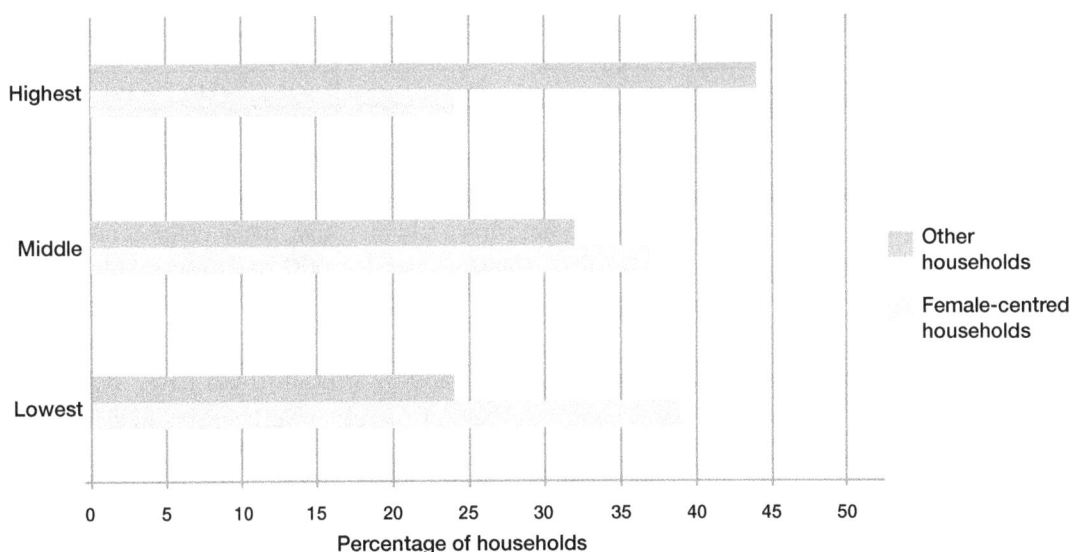

Given the low levels of employment income, it is not surprising that the occupational profile of the sample is dominated by those in unskilled and semi-skilled categories of work (Table 10). Of those in formal or informal employment, over half (54%) were working in unskilled or semi-skilled jobs, including domestic service (18%), manual labour (18%) and services (11%). Around 27% were in skilled jobs (mostly skilled manual jobs, primarily in manufacturing). Within that group, the number of better-paid professionals, office workers and civil servants was relatively small.

TABLE 10: Occupational Profile		
Occupation	No.	%
Skilled	146	26.6
Manual workers	87	15.9
Office workers	17	3.1
Teachers	13	2.4
Professionals	9	1.6
Health workers	8	1.4
Managers/supervisors	6	1.1
Civil servants	6	1.1
Semi-skilled/unskilled	294	53.6
Domestic workers	99	18.1
Manual workers	97	17.7
Service workers	60	10.9
Security/police	26	4.7
Farmworkers	12	2.2
Truck drivers	7	1.2
Self-employed	47	8.6
SMME entrepreneurs	30	5.5
Informal traders/hawkers	17	3.1
Other	61	11.1

The other striking feature of the household employment profile is how few households obtain income from the informal economy. For the 8% of households that participate in the informal economy, the average income is just R13,488 per annum or slightly over R1,000 per month. Other studies of Msunduzi help to explain the low rate of participation in the informal economy. One begins by painting a rather optimistic picture of a vibrant informal economy: the CBD and its arterial streets have "dense informal activities" and large numbers of people have been pushed into the informal economy in order to survive.[32] At the same time, the report notes that the informal economy in Msunduzi is small compared to other cities and that the data is sparse.[33] In 2006, another study noted that there were only 2,500 informal traders in the city but that even then competition for space in the city centre was intense.[34] Two thirds of businesses in the informal economy were estimated to earn less than R1,000 per month.[35] The ILO reports that the municipal response to informality has been "inconsistent and contradictory" and that the pro-growth strategy of the city by-passes informal entrepreneurs.[36] The money earned is barely enough even to warrant the label "survivalist" and can be more accurately described as "disguised unemployment."[37]

4. LEVELS OF FOOD INSECURITY

The AFSUN survey used four international cross-cultural scales developed by the Food and Nutrition Technical Assistance Project (FANTA) to assess levels of food insecurity in the poorer neighbourhoods of Southern African cities:

Household Food Insecurity Access Scale (HFIAS): The HFIAS measures the degree of food insecurity during the month prior to the survey.[38] An HFIAS score is calculated for each household based on answers to nine "frequency-of-occurrence" questions. The minimum score is 0 and the maximum is 27. The higher the score, the more food insecurity the household experienced.

Household Food Insecurity Access Prevalence Indicator (HFIAP): The HFIAP indicator uses the responses to the HFIAS questions to group households into four levels of household food insecurity: food secure, mildly food insecure, moderately food insecure and severely food insecure.

Household Dietary Diversity Scale (HDDS): Dietary diversity refers to how many food groups are consumed within the household in the previous 24 hours.[39] The maximum number, based on the FAO classification of food groups for Africa, is 12. An increase in the average number of different food groups consumed provides a quantifiable measure of improved household food access.

Months of Adequate Household Food Provisioning Indicator (MAHFP): The MAHFP indicator captures changes in the household's ability to ensure that food is available above a minimum level all year round.[40] Households are asked to identify in which months (during the past 12 months) they did not have access to sufficient food to meet their household needs.

The mean HFIAS score for the Msunduzi households was 11.3 (with a median of 11), which indicates high overall levels of food insecurity (Cape Town, for example, averaged 10.7 and Johannesburg 5.7) (Table

11). Just four of the 11 SADC cities surveyed (Manzini, Harare, Maseru and Lusaka) had worse scores than Msunduzi. Nearly 30% of the Msunduzi households had HFIAS scores of 15 or above and 13% had scores of 20 or above.

TABLE 11: Msunduzi HFIAS Scores Compared to Other Cities

	Mean HFIAS	Median HFIAS	No.
Manzini, Swaziland	14.9	14.7	489
Harare, Zimbabwe	14.7	16.0	454
Maseru, Lesotho	12.8	13.0	795
Lusaka, Zambia	11.5	11.0	386
Msunduzi, South Africa	11.3	11.0	548
Gaborone, Botswana	10.8	11.0	391
Cape Town, South Africa	10.7	11.0	1,026
Maputo, Mozambique	10.4	10.0	389
Windhoek, Namibia	9.3	9.0	436
Blantyre, Malawi	5.3	3.7	431
Johannesburg, South Africa	4.7	1.5	976

HFIAS scores varied significantly with a number of variables including household structure, size and income (Table 12). Female-centred households had the highest scores, averaging 12.2, and are therefore most food insecure. Nuclear households were the least food insecure with an average HFIAS of only 9.5. Household size also affected the HFIAS scores: the largest households (<10 members) averaged 14.3 compared to 10.9 for the smaller households (with 1–5 members). Finally, income has a clear influence on household food security. Households in the lowest income tercile scored 14.5 compared with only 8.4 amongst those in the upper tercile.

TABLE 12: HFIAS by Household Type, Size and Income

	Mean HFIAS	No. of households
Household type		
Female-centred	12.2	291
Male-centred	11.1	65
Extended	10.7	74
Nuclear	9.5	118
Household size		
>10	14.3	25
6–10	11.7	178
1–5	10.9	345
Income terciles		
Lowest	14.5	143
Middle	12.2	159
Highest	8.4	150

The HFIAP scale adds nuance to the analysis but confirms that the Msunduzi households experience very high levels of food insecurity. As many as 60% of the households were classified as severely food insecure on the HFIAP with another 27% moderately food insecure (Table 13). Only 7% of households were completely food secure. Msunduzi compares more favourably with other cities on the HFIAP, with seven cities having more severely food insecure households (including Cape Town). However, only five cities have a greater proportion of food secure households. Only Harare, Lusaka, Maputo, Maseru and Manzini have fewer food secure households than Msunduzi.

TABLE 13: Msunduzi HFIAP Scores Compared to Other Cities				
	Food insecure (%)			Food secure (%)
	Severe	Moderate	Mild	
Manzini, Swaziland	79	13	3	6
Harare, Zimbabwe	72	24	3	2
Lusaka, Zambia	69	24	3	4
Cape Town, South Africa	68	12	5	15
Maseru, Lesotho	65	25	6	5
Gaborone, Botswana	63	19	6	12
Windhoek, Namibia	63	14	5	18
Msunduzi, South Africa	60	27	6	7
Maputo, Mozambique	54	32	9	5
Johannesburg, South Africa	27	15	14	44
Blantyre, Malawi	21	30	15	34

As with the HFIAS, there are significant differences in the HFIAP scores within the survey sample (Table 14). For example, female-centred households experience greater food insecurity than other households: 64% are severely food insecure compared with 56% of other households. Or again, only 5% of female-centred households classified as food secure compared to 9% of all other households. Household size does not appear to have as strong a relationship with food security on the HFIAP with only minor differences between households with five or less and more than five members. The exception is the largest households (>10) with very high levels of severe food insecurity. Income exercises the greatest effect on levels of food insecurity (Figure 6). As many as 78% of households in the lowest income bracket are severely food insecure and only 2% are food secure or mildly food insecure. This compares with equivalent figures of 44% and 22% amongst households in the upper income bracket. There should be cause for concern that so many of the relatively better off households (most of which have a wage worker) are still so food insecure since this indicates that current incomes are insufficient to protect many from food insecurity.

TABLE 14: HFIAP Scores by Household Type, Size and Income

	Food insecure (%)			Food secure (%)	N
	Severe	Moderate	Mild		
Household type					
Female-centred	64	27	4	5	291
Other households	56	27	8	9	257
Household size					
1–5	59	26	7	8	345
6–10	58	31	5	7	178
>10	88	4	0	8	25
Income terciles					
Lowest	78	21	1	1	143
Middle	64	28	4	4	159
Highest	44	34	11	11	150

FIGURE 6: Food Security Status by Household Income

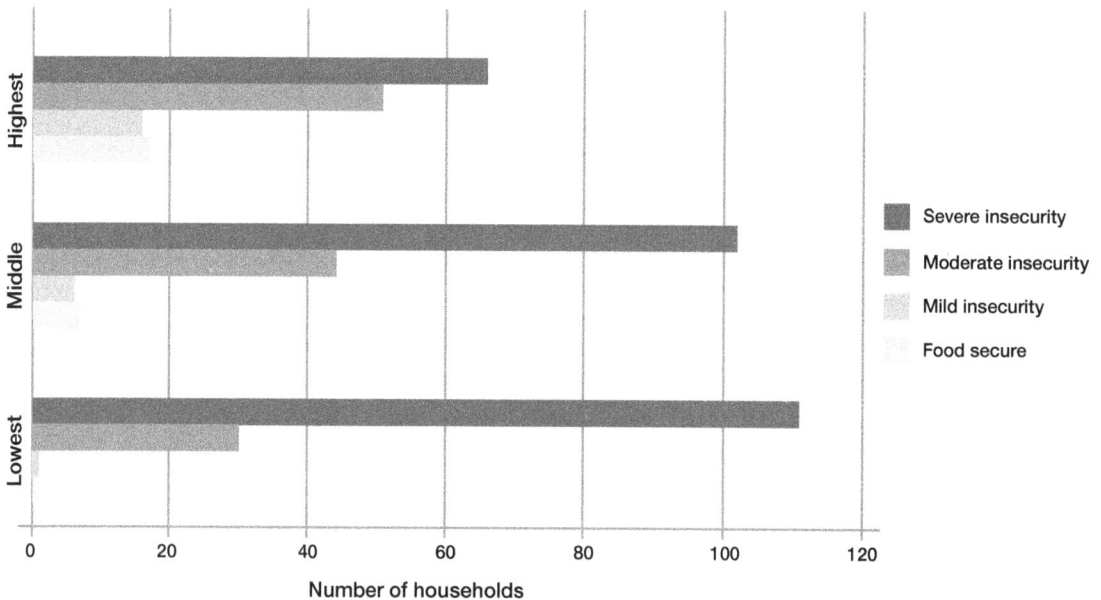

The HDDS scale addresses the dietary quality component of food insecurity. The mean HDDS for the survey households was 5.5 out of a possible 12, which means that in the 24 hours prior to the survey the average household ate food from six of the 12 major African food groups. In total, over half of the households (53%) ate from five or fewer food groups (Figure 7). The most common groups included cereals (primarily maize), sugars, oils and fats, and roots and tubers (mainly potatoes) (Table 15). Over 40% had eaten vegetables and meat or poultry but, in general, the diet is not particularly diverse and is heavy in fats, sugars and starch.

FIGURE 7: Distribution of Dietary Diversity Scores

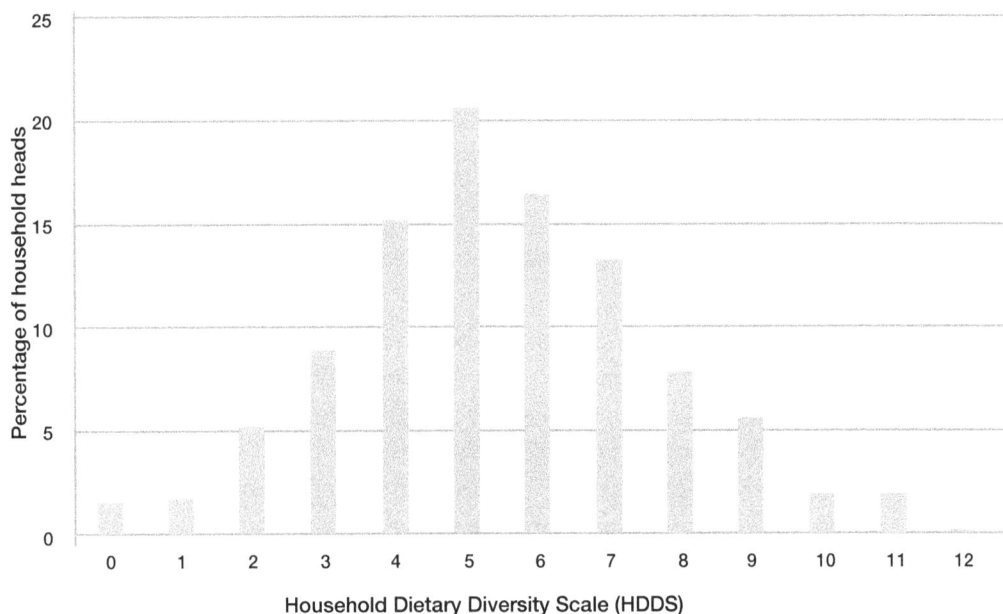

TABLE 15: Foods Consumed by Households in Previous 24 Hours

Food groups	% of households
Cereals/grain	96
Sugar/honey	80
Oils/fats/butter	61
Roots/tubers	53
Vegetables	47
Meat/poultry	42
Beans/peas/lentils/nuts	21
Milk/cheese/milk products	21
Eggs	17
Fish	8

The answers to questions about household responses to food insecurity provide further insights into food availability, dietary quality and the satisfaction of food preferences (Table 16). The first question was whether the head of the household had ever worried that the household would not have enough food during the previous month. Around half (51%) had sometimes/often been worried about this, while only a quarter had never had such worries. To what extent did worrying about the lack of food translate into actually going without? Fewer, but still a third, said their household had sometimes/often had no food to eat of any kind because of lack of resources (around half had never experienced this level of deprivation.) A smaller number said that members of their households had sometimes/often gone to bed hungry or gone a whole day and night without food (21% and 16% respectively). The difference in prevalence between not having food and the experience of hunger suggests that households are able to obtain food from other sources even when they cannot purchase it.

The next set of questions related to dietary diversity and food preferences. Here, the majority of households were dissatisfied on all counts. For example, 58% said that the household had sometimes/often eaten a limited variety of foods due to a lack of resources (only 20% had never had this experience). An even higher number (64%) said that the household members were sometimes/often unable to eat the kinds of foods they preferred because of a lack of resources (only 16% were able to satisfy their preferences). Finally, 60% had sometimes/often eaten foods that they really did not want to eat because of a lack of resources with which to obtain other types of food. Taken together, these answers confirm the quantitative picture painted by the HDDS of extremely limited dietary diversity for the majority of households.

TABLE 16: Experience of Food Insecurity		
	Often/ Sometimes	Rarely/ Never
Worried that household would not have enough food	51	49
No food due to absence of resources to obtain it	32	68
Gone to sleep hungry	20	78
Gone without food for a whole day and night	16	84
Ate smaller meal than needed	54	46
Ate fewer meals in day	45	55
Ate limited variety of foods	58	42
Unable to eat preferred foods due to lack of resources	64	36
Ate undesirable foods	60	40

The fourth FANTA food security scale (the Months of Adequate Household Provisioning or MAHFP index) aims to assess whether households can access a regular supply of food throughout the year (Figure 8). A total of 69% of the Msunduzi households said that there were months of the year in which they had an inadequate food supply. The majority of these households (65%) had an inadequate supply of food for 1-3 months of the year, while 14% had inadequate food for 4-6 months of the year. The remaining 19% had inadequate food for more than six months a year (with 15% having an inadequate supply throughout the year). Overall, the average for the surveyed households as a whole was 9.18 (of months of adequate provisioning). Over the course of the year, there are two periods when the number of households with inadequate food provisioning rises (Figure 8): December and January (the holiday season) and June to September (the winter months before the harvest).

FIGURE 8: Number of Households with Inadequate Food Provisioning Each Month

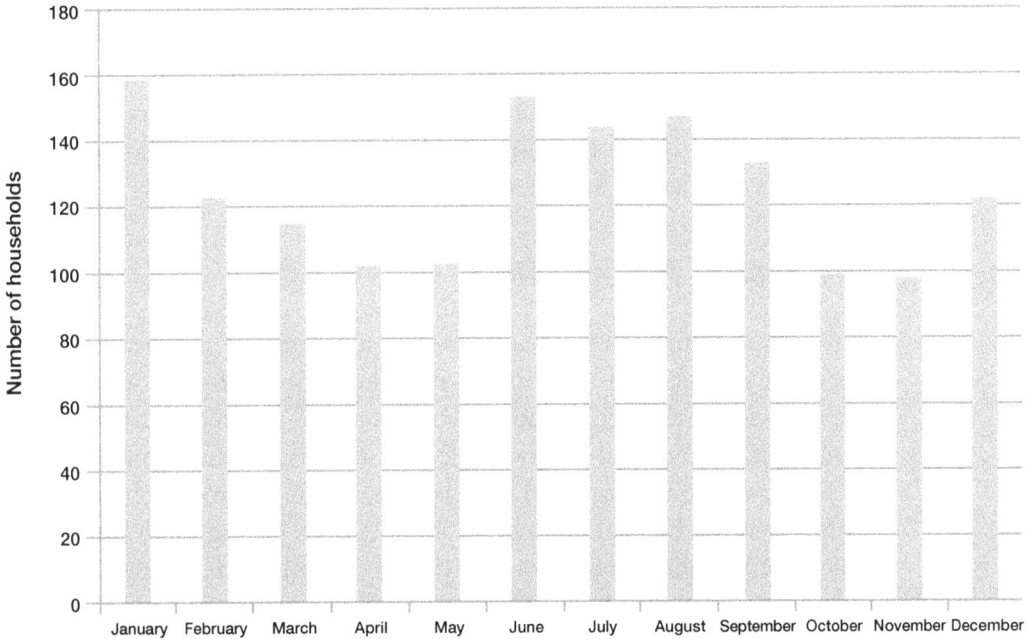

The marked seasonal pattern in the HFIAP suggests that urban households are dependent to some degree on the rural agricultural cycle or seasonality in urban agriculture. This raises the obvious question of whether, and to what degree, poor Msunduzi households source their food from the rural areas or through home production in the form of urban agriculture. More generally, given the extremely high levels of food insecurity amongst the urban poor, it is necessary to ask to what extent households are dependent for their food on market versus non-market sources. Certainly, both the HFIAP and HFIAS scores suggest that there is a significant relationship between food security and household income. Does this imply that households buy most of their food? For, if so, this means that the problem of food insecurity in Msunduzi is a problem of inadequate income or high food prices or both. Furthermore, if households are purchasing most of their food, then what outlets do they patronize and why? This report has already established that only a small minority of surveyed households actually participate in the informal food economy. Does this mean that the informal economy is not a major source of food, as it is in many other Southern African cities?

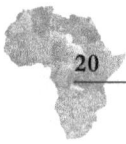

5. NON-MARKET FOOD SOURCING

In Southern African cities, there are generally three major ways that a household can access food outside the market and without incurring cash expenditure: urban agriculture, informal rural–urban food transfers and obtaining food from other households in the community (through begging or borrowing or sharing meals).

5.1 Urban Agriculture

Urban agriculture has been advocated as a potentially significant way of ensuring greater food security for poor households in Msunduzi. This is premised on the belief that newcomers to the city have rural farming skills that can be used to good effect in the city.[41] Furthermore, there are fewer constraints on land than in other large urban centres in South Africa, with individual households in most cases having some land available around their houses for cultivation.[42] To what extent, then, are the households surveyed by AFSUN using this and other available land, as well as their agricultural skills, to engage in food production? Amongst this group of poor urban households, the answer is "very little." Asked where they normally obtain their food, only 11% of the heads said that the household grows some of it. The understanding of the word "normally" here is critical since answers to other questions suggest greater levels of participation in urban agriculture. For example, 30% of households said that they eat food that they have grown themselves during the course of the year. However, when this group is broken down by the frequency with which they eat homegrown food, only 14% do so on a regular basis (at least once a week). Hence, "normally" seems to signify very regular (at least weekly) consumption. The other 16% grow some food but eat it much less frequently. Of those growing food, the vast majority (84%) were doing so in their own gardens. There seems to be little of the kind of field agriculture on public and private open space seen in cities such as Harare and Lusaka.[43]

5.2 Rural-Urban Food Transfers

AFSUN found that an important food source for poor urban households in many cities is the transfer of foodstuffs from relatives (and, to a lesser extent, friends) living outside the city in question.[44] In general, these transfers were either from the rural areas where the relatives live and farm or from other urban areas where they live and work. Rural–urban transfers of food turned out to be far more important than urban–urban transfers. However, the volume of these informal food transfers, the frequency with which they occur and the types of produce transferred varied considerably from city to city.

In cities such as Windhoek, Lusaka and Harare, over 40% of households receive food from outside the city from relatives and friends. In these cities, virtually all of the transfers are from the rural areas. In the case of the three South African cities in the survey, the proportion of households receiving food transfers is very much lower (14% in Johannesburg, 18% in Cape Town and 24% in Msunduzi). There are at least two likely reasons for the lower South African figures. First, South Africa is easily the most urbanized of all the countries and many urbanites have tenuous links with the rural areas and few, if any, family members living there. Second, rural agriculture by smallholders in South Africa is in an advanced state of disintegration. Rural families do not produce enough to feed themselves, much less send food to relatives in the towns.

FIGURE 9: Total Food Transfers to Urban Households (% of Households)

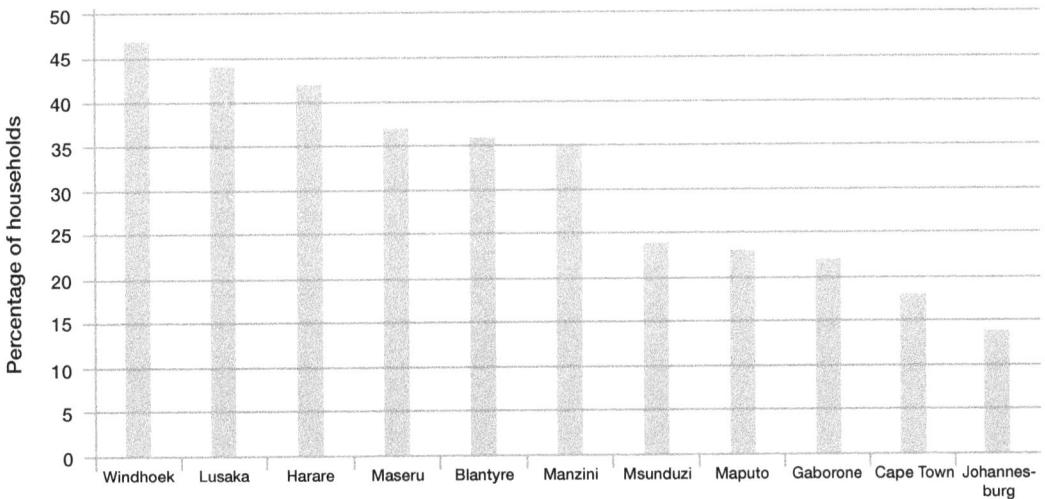

A quarter of the surveyed households in Msunduzi receive food from family and friends outside the city, but where does the food come from, how often is it sent and do the transfers improve dietary diversity and alleviate food insecurity? In fact, only 4% of households in Msunduzi had received food from relatives and friends in the rural areas in the previous year. In other words, informal rural-urban food transfers are unimportant in the city. The other 20% received transfers from family and friends living in other urban areas. This confirms the earlier observations about the impact of high levels of urbanization and rural agricultural underdevelopment.

At the same time, it does point to an interesting phenomenon requiring further research: that is, the existence of informal food networks linking cities and households in different cities. The kinds of foods transferred tended to conform to the main food groups already found in Msunduzi – cereals, potatoes, meat and poultry, and vegetables. In other words, the food is transferred primarily to make up shortfalls in the existing food basket rather than diversifying or improving the quality of the diet.

5.3 Food Sharing

Research elsewhere in urban Africa shows that poor households tend to be more open to sharing what food they have with neighbours and others in the community who are in greater need.[45] The issue of inter-household food transfers is under-researched in Southern Africa. The AFSUN survey provided empirical evidence that inter-household food sharing is a relatively common phenomenon in poor urban neighbourhoods. Across the 11 cities, 21% of households said they share meals with neighbours and other households. The same proportion said they borrow food from others and 20% that they consume food provided by neighbours and other households. These three elements of inter-household food transfers – sharing, borrowing and donations – are a normal source of food for one in five households.

In Msunduzi, the figure is closer to one in 10. Six percent said that they normally obtain food through meal sharing, 8% through borrowing and 7% through donations. In the week prior to the survey, however, the equivalent figures were 9%, 12% and 12%. The survey was undertaken at a time when food prices had been escalating, causing greater hardship and food insecurity (see page 26), which may explain the difference between the two sets of figures. Only 2% of households said they engaged in any of the forms of inter-household transfer on a continuous basis (at least five days a week) (Table 17). Although less than 2% of households benefit from any of the forms of transfers at least five days a week, 8–10% obtain food in this manner at least once a week and the same number at least once a month. Occasional transfers (once or twice a year) are almost non-existent.

TABLE 17: Inter-Household Transfers of Food			
	Sharing meals	Borrowing food	Donated food
Normal source of food	6.2	8.4	7.2
In week prior to survey	8.8	11.8	12.4
Daily	1.1	1.7	1.5
Weekly	6.6	10.3	9.2
Monthly	8.5	10.7	8.3
Once every six months	1.1	0.7	1.1
Annual	0.4	0.2	0.0
Never	82.4	76.4	79.1

6. MARKET SOURCES OF FOOD

The previous section demonstrated that the majority of poor urban households in Msunduzi do not source any food from urban agriculture, rural–urban transfers or inter-household transfers. Almost all households buy the vast majority of the food they consume, a pattern observed in both of the other South African cities and, indeed, throughout the region as a whole. What distinguishes Msunduzi from many other cities, however, is the extraordinarily high levels of reliance on supermarkets, especially compared with the informal food economy. To better understand the market-based food sourcing strategies of Msunduzi households, it is necessary to understand the nature of the urban food system and, in particular, its domination by formal retailing.

Across the region, supermarket expansion is dramatically changing the way in which food is delivered to the city, the type and variety of foods available for purchase, and the pricing of food.[46] In the 11 cities as a whole, 79% of households use supermarkets as a source of food; in Msunduzi, the equivalent figure is 97%, or almost every household whatever its income, size, structure or degree of food insecurity. The fact that only 40% of households source food from smaller outlets (compared to 68% for the AFSUN sample as a whole) suggests that supermarkets may have had a significantly negative impact on the viability of the small independent food retail sector.[47]

TABLE 18: Food Outlets Normally Patronized by Poor Urban Households		
	Msunduzi (% of households)	SADC region* (% of households)
Supermarkets	97	79
Informal food sector	42	72
Small retail outlets	40	68
*AFSUN data from 11 SADC cities		

6.1 Supermarkets

Msunduzi has an extremely high concentration of supermarkets for a city of its size. A 2010 study of the supermarket sector showed that all of the major South African chains are well-represented: Pick n Pay (3 outlets), Shoprite Checkers (4), Spar (7) and Woolworths (4).[48] The study also profiles a local company, Save Cash and Carry, with two outlets. The supermarkets owned by the major chains are integrated into centralized procurement and distribution systems, sourcing their produce via company distribution centres in Msunduzi or Durban, rather than directly from local producers. Spar outlets are locally-owned franchise operations and they, together with Save Cash and Carry, do source some fresh produce from local suppliers (primarily white commercial farms) and from the Mkondeni Municipality Market.[49] There is little evidence that rural smallholders supply any of the produce sold in supermarkets. The report notes that none of the major supermarkets are located in poorer urban neighbourhoods, although there are a number of small, locally-owned supermarkets in some of these communities.

FIGURE 10: The Location of Supermarkets within Msunduzi Municipality

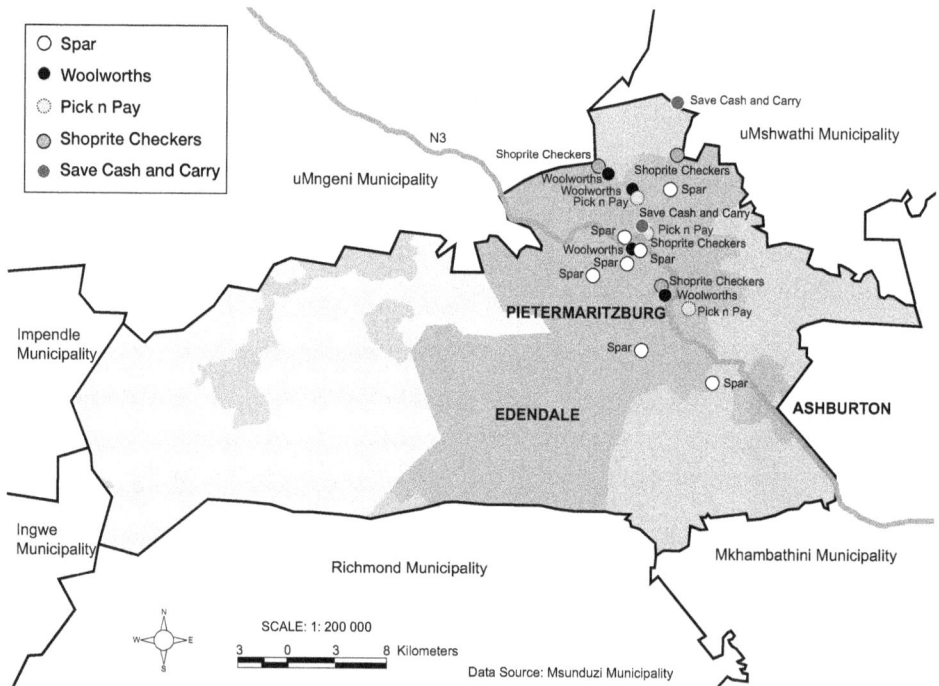

As noted above, almost all poor households in Msunduzi shop at super-markets. Most (76%) tend to source food from these outlets on a month-ly basis, which tends to coincide with the payment of social grants and monthly wages. In an increasing number of South African cities, social grants are actually paid out at supermarkets.[50] The monthly pattern of patronage suggests that households obtain non-perishable items and sta-ples in bulk at supermarkets. The 20% of households who shop at super-markets at least once a week are probably also buying meat, chicken and vegetables there. Small retail outlets (which would include grocers and butcheries) are patronized more frequently than supermarkets (31% at least once a week) as a source of fresh produce.

TABLE 19: Frequency of Patronage of Major Food Sources			
	Supermarkets (% of households)	Small retail (% of households)	Informal economy (% of households)
Daily	1.5	13.1	6.4
Weekly	18.8	17.5	20.8
Monthly	75.9	8.8	13.6
Every six months	0.4	0.6	1.1
Annually	0.2	0.4	0.2
Never	3.3	59.7	57.9

6.2 Informal Food Economy

There is considerable debate about the impact of supermarkets on the informal food economy. As noted above, very few of the surveyed house-holds participate in the informal economy. Only 42% of households in Msunduzi source food from the informal economy, compared with 72% across the 11 cities as a whole. The informal food system in Msunduzi appears to be significantly smaller than in many other cities in the region. This could be because of intense competition from supermarkets but more research would be needed to test this proposition.

In many South African cities, municipal fresh produce markets are a sig-nificant source of fruit and vegetables for informal vendors. In Msunduzi, however, the fresh produce market is a considerable distance from the CBD and is not on direct public transport routes.[51] Individual buyers are also unable to negotiate lower prices with selling agents who are only prepared to give discounts for bulk buying. As a result of these various constraints, informal food retailers generally prefer to buy from supermar-kets and wholesalers in or close to the CBD.

One supermarket company, the local Save Cash and Carry, runs a training programme in business techniques for informal traders.[52] However, none of the big corporates appear to do anything of this nature to encourage small entrepreneurs. Nearly 60% of poor households in Msunduzi never source food from the informal economy, one of the highest figures in the region. Only 6% of households buy food from informal traders, hawkers and street-food sellers on a daily basis, which again is quite different from patterns of frequent patronage in other cities.

7. IMPACT OF FOOD PRICE INCREASES

Given that the vast majority of poor urban households in Msunduzi buy most of their food, the degree of food security is likely to be unusually sensitive to increases in the price of staple foods in the supermarkets and, to a lesser degree, on the streets. The AFSUN surveys were implemented during the global food price increases of 2008. Research literature has shown that these increases caused considerable hardship for poor urban households across the region and continent.[53] The final section of this paper therefore examines the impact on the food security of the poor of Msunduzi.

Household heads were first asked to compare the economic condition of their household at the time of the survey with the situation a year previously. Nearly three quarters (71%) said that it was worse/much worse. Only 11% registered an improvement in their household situation. While not all of this deterioration may be attributable to rising food prices, the fact that this negative evaluation was so pervasive amongst all types of household suggests that this is a significant part of the explanation. At the time of the survey, mean household income was R24,420 and mean household expenditures on food were R8,136 (or 33% of total expenditure). Given that a significant proportion of the rest of the income goes on necessary expenses such as transportation, fuel, school fees, medical expenses and housing, a sudden increase in food prices will inevitably have a major impact on household budgets.

The survey asked two basic questions about the impact of food price increases on food security: How frequently had the household gone without food due to price increases in the previous six months? And what types of food had they gone without? Very few households (just 13%) had been unaffected by the food price increases (Table 20). The proportion of unaffected female-centred households was slightly lower than the proportion of other households (12% versus 16%). Forty percent of female-centred households were affected on a daily basis or several times a week, compared with 35% of other types of households. In other words, while a large number of households of all types were going without food, female-centred households were even more badly affected.

TABLE 20: Frequency of Going Without Food Due to Prices Increases		
	Female-centred (% of households)	Other (% of households)
Every day	23.4	21.9
Between 2–6 days a week	16.5	12.9
Once a week	14.0	13.3
Once a month	33.5	35.2
Never	12.2	16.0

The consumption of food in all food groups was affected by the increase in food prices (Table 21). However, the proportion of households who were affected varied considerably from a high of 69% for milk and milk products to a low of 25% for sugar or honey. Around 44% of affected households reduced their consumption of food staples of maize/bread and 47% their consumption of vegetables. What is most striking, however, is that the food groups most affected were precisely those which would ensure dietary diversity and a more balanced diet (milk and milk products, eggs, fish, meat, poultry and fruit). In other words, food price increases not only affect the quantity of food consumed but the quality of the household diet.

TABLE 21: Foods Gone Without Due to Price Increases	
	% of affected households
Milk and milk products	69.1
Eggs	65.2
Fish	65.1
Meat and poultry	65.0
Fruits	63.1
Foods with beans, peas, lentils, nuts	51.1
Vegetables	46.8
Cereals	43.9
Foods with oils and fats	34.5
Roots and tubers	27.4
Sugar or honey	24.9

8. CONCLUSIONS AND RECOMMENDATIONS

Msunduzi is a city in which there is plenty of food but where the majority of the urban poor regularly go hungry. The AFSUN survey found that 60% of households in poor Msunduzi neighbourhoods are severely food insecure and another 27% are moderately food secure. Only 7% could be considered food secure. The survey results show that the urban poor in Msunduzi are significantly worse off than their counterparts in Cape Town (15% food secure) and Johannesburg (44% food secure). A third of the households reported that they sometimes or often have no food to eat of any kind. The situation was just as bad on other indicators: 58% eat a limited variety of foods due to a lack of resources, 54% eat smaller meals than they need and 45% cut back on the number of meals for the same reason. Dietary diversity was also extremely low. Food insecurity is clearly related to levels of income even in poor communities (with 78% of those in the lowest income band and 44% of those in the upper band experiencing severe food insecurity). Household size did not make a great deal of difference to levels of insecurity but female-centred households are more food insecure than male-centred households (64% versus 56% severely food insecure).

Msunduzi is a classic case study of a city whose food supply system is dominated by modern supermarket supply chains. The informal food economy is relatively small, urban agriculture is not especially significant and informal rural-urban food transfers are lower than in many other cities surveyed. In this respect, Msunduzi offers the other cities a picture of their own future. Supermarket expansion is occurring at an extremely rapid rate throughout Southern Africa, tying urban spaces and populations into global, regional and national supply chains. While supermarkets offer greater variety and fresher produce than many other outlets, they clearly do not meet the needs of the poor. Their pricing structures and profit margins are such that poor households in Msunduzi tend to patronize them only on payday and social grants payout day when they buy staples in bulk. However, unlike in other cities where "food deserts" are watered to some degree by vibrant informal food systems that make food more accessible to the urban poor on a daily basis, Msunduzi residents struggle to access informal sources.[54] Only 42% of surveyed households reported that they normally obtain food through informal channels, compared to 72% for the region as a whole.

The high levels of unemployment coupled with the absence of a vibrant

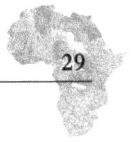

informal economy, especially when compared to other Southern African cities, is a major threat to food security for Msunduzi's urban poor. The population of Msunduzi is primarily young and a significant number of young adults are unemployed. In addition, the poor adult population has no or little education and lacks the necessary skills to access better paying jobs. The AFSUN data confirms that recent improvements in the economy did not reach poorer households. The current IDP, however, seems to accommodate poorer households in new local economic development plans for it provides, inter alia, for creation of jobs and income opportunities as well as support for the informal economic sector, including trading space and training programmes for informal trade.[55] Implementation of these plans should at least provide poor households with improved employment opportunities or alternative and additional livelihood strategies in the informal economy.

Both census data and the AFSUN survey confirm that female-centred households are the dominant type in the poorer areas of the city. In addition, the AFSUN data indicates that these households are more vulnerable to food insecurity. Significantly, only 15% of females were in full-time employment as opposed to 28% of males and, where women did work, their average annual earnings were lower. The Msunduzi study confirms the regional AFSUN findings on gender and food insecurity.[56] For female-centred households, the fundamental food insecurity determinants include low incomes and unemployment. These employment and wage-based gender differences have a long history and require national government intervention in areas such as education for girls, review of wage legislation and policies, as well as a gender bias in favour of women in the implementation of Employment Equity legislation. In the short term, however, the role of the social protection system needs examination.

The Msunduzi study found that a large number of households were accessing social grants and that these served as their sole source of cash income. While this illustrates the importance of social grants for the survival of poor households, one needs to ask why this particular strategy does not guarantee food security. Part of the reason is that the social grants are relatively small and insufficient to meet all of the competing draws on limited household income. They may take the edge off hunger but they do not eliminate food insecurity. The impact of low and irregular income is compounded by the high and rising cost of food. Here the pricing strategies of supermarkets become extremely important and need much closer scrutiny. Some corporates are examining the possibility of incorporating small farmers into their supply chains but this food security strategy is unlikely to benefit more than a few and is highly unlikely to affect prices at the till. Others make unsold food available to food banks and NGOs, which is certainly far more desirable than dumping.[57] However, these are essentially band-aid measures. Corporate responsibility towards food security in South African cities needs to be looked at afresh. Supermarket chains may feel that they have no particular responsibility to their poor urban consumers but they are an essential part of the solution to urban food insecurity in the country.

ENDNOTES

1   For legislation and a history of the municipal boundaries see Municipal Demarcation Board at www.demarcation.org.za; see also L. Piper and R.Deacon, "Party Politics, Elite Accountability and Public Participation: Ward Committee Politics in the Msunduzi Municipality" *Transformation* 66/67 (2008): 61-82.

2   *Census 2011: Municipal Report KwaZulu-Natal*, Report No. 03-01-53, Statistics South Africa, Pretoria, 2012.

3   G. Robbins and S. Hobbs, "Cities with Jobs – Confronting the Employment Challenge: An Examination of Approaches to Employment in Two South African Case Study Cities" Employment Working Paper No. 127, International Labour Office, Geneva, 2012, p. 37.

4   J. Smith and M. Green, "Free Basic Water in Msunduzi, KwaZulu-Natal : Is It Making a Difference to the Lives of Low-Income Households?" *Water Policy* 7 (2005): 443-67; I. Chetty, "The Free Basic Electricity Policy: A Case Study of Policy Implementation in the Msunduzi Municipality" M.Soc.Sci. Thesis, University of KwaZulu-Natal, 2006; C. Sutton, "Urban Open Space: A Case Study of Msunduzi Municipality, South Africa" M.Env.Stud. Thesis, Queen's University, 2008; K. Naidoo, "An Analysis of Municipal Solid Waste Management in South Africa using the Msunduzi Municipality as a Case Study" MSc Thesis, University of KwaZulu-Natal, 2009; A. Goebel, B. Dodson and T. Hill, "Urban Advantage or Urban Penalty? A Case Study of Female-Headed Households in a South African City" *Health and Place* 16 (2010): 573-80; S. Zondi, "Evaluation of the Implementation of Water and Sanitation Policies in a Low-Cost Housing Settlement of Ambleton and Ambleton Extension in Pietermaritzburg, Msunduzi Municipality, M.Env.Dev. Thesis, University of KwaZulu-Natal, 2010; A. Goebel and B. Dodson, "Housing and Marginality for Female-Headed Households: Observations from Msunduzi Municipality (Pietermaritzburg, South Africa)" *Canadian Journal of African Studies* 45(2011): 240-72; M. Boakye and O. Akpor, "Stakeholders' Participation in Water Management: A Case Study of the Msunduzi Catchment Management" *Journal of Sustainable Development* 5 (2012): 104-12.

5   For example, U. Bob, "Rural African Women, Food (In) security and Agricultural Production in the Ekuthuleni Land Redistribution Project, KwaZulu-Natal" Agenda 51(2002): 16-32; S. Hendriks, "Unfair Burden: Women's Risks and Vulnerability to Food Insecurity" *Agenda* 51(2002): 51-7; S. Kaschula, "Using People to Cope with the Hunger: Social Networks and Food Transfers Amongst HIV/AIDS Afflicted Households in KwaZulu-Natal, South Africa" *AIDS and Behavior* 15(2011): 1490-502.

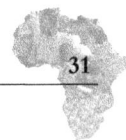

6   Msunduzi Municipality, *Integrated Development Plan 2011-2016 and Beyond: Isixaxa/ Pulling Together*, Msunduzi, 2010, p. 21.

7   SRK Consulting, *Msunduzi Municipality: Draft Strategic Environmental Assessment*, Report No. 376998/DSEA, March 2010.

8   Ibid., p. 37.

9   Ibid., pp. 47,57.

10   J. Crush and B. Frayne, " Urban Food Security and the New International Food Security Agenda" *Development Southern Africa* 28(4) (2011): 527-44.

11   For more details of the methodology see B. Frayne et al, *The State of Urban Food Insecurity in Southern Africa*, AFSUN Urban Food Security Series No 2, Cape Town.

12   *Census 2011: Municipal Report KwaZulu-Natal.*

13   Ibid., Tables 5.1.4.1 to 5.1.4.4.

14   Ibid., Table 5.1.1.11

15   J. Crush, B. Frayne and M. McLachlan, *Rapid Urbanization and the Nutrition Transition in Southern Africa*, AFSUN Urban Food Security Series No 7, Cape Town, 2011.

16   J. Crush, S. Drimie, B. Frayne and M. Caesar, "The HIV and Urban Food Security Nexus in Africa" *Food Security* 3 (2011): 347-62.

17   M. Ferreira, M., Keikelame and Y. Mosaval, "Older Women as Carers to Children and Grandchildren Affected by AIDS" Institute of Ageing in Africa, University of Cape Town, Cape Town, 2001; C. Ogunmefun, "The Impacts of Adult HIV/AIDS Mortality on Elderly Women and Their Households in Rural South Africa" PhD Thesis, University of Witwatersrand, 2008.

18   Built Environment Support Group (BESG), "The Msunduzi HIV/AIDS Strategy: A Partnership Response to HIV/AIDS at Local Government Level" Report for Msunduzi Municipality, Msunduzi, 2003. The strategy's effectiveness is evaluated in T. Makhathini, "Municipal Responses to HIV and AIDS: A Case Study of uMgungundlovu District and Four of its Local Municipalities in KwaZulu-Natal" M.A. Thesis, University of Witwatersrand, 2010, pp. 71-9.

19   *Census 2011: Municipal Report KwaZulu-Natal*, Table 5.4.1.1

20   J. Van Zyl, C. Cross and M. O'Donovan, "Overview of the Extent and Nature of the Unbundling of South African Households and the Implications Thereof" Report Commissioned by the Presidency, Pretoria, 2008.

21   Female- and male-centred households are households with a woman/man as head, with no spouse or partner due to death/separation/divorce/abandonment. A nuclear household comprises immediate blood relatives (usually male-headed with a spouse or partner), while an extended household includes immediate and distant relatives (also usually male-headed).

22   *Census 2011: Municipal Report KwaZulu-Natal*, Table 5.4.10.1

23   *Census 2011: Municipal Report KwaZulu-Natal*, Table 5.1.7.1

24   Ibid.

25   N. Naidoo, "Msunduzi Housing Shortage: 'A Timebomb'" *Natal Witness* 2 October 2012. Other sources claim that 70,000 people live in informal settlements; see Goebel and Dodson, "Housing and Marginality" p. 255.

26   A. Goebel, "Sustainable Urban Development? Low-Cost Housing Challenges

in South Africa" *Habitat International* 31 (2007): 291-302; P. Karemera, "Implementing Environmental Policy Requirements in Low-Cost Housing in South Africa: A Case Study of Msunduzi Municipality" M.Env.Dev. Thesis, University of KwaZulu-Natal, 2007; M. Mwanamwenge, "Evolving Stakeholder Roles and Perceptions of Sustainability of Low Cost Housing Developments in Msunduzi Municipality: The Case of Ambleton" M.Env.Dev. Thesis, University of KwaZulu-Natal, 2007.

27 Robbins and Hobbs, "Cities with Jobs" p. 38.

28 Ibid., p. 42.

29 Ibid., p. 45.

30 *Census 2011: Municipal Report KwaZulu-Natal*, Table 5.3.1.1.

31 Ibid., Table 5.4.9.1.

32 T. Quazi. "An Analysis of Municipal Approaches to Incorporating The Informal Economy into the Urban Fabric: A Comparative Study of Msunduzi Local Municipality (Pietermaritzburg) and Hibiscus Coast Municipality (Port Shepstone)" M.Dev.Stud. Thesis, University of KwaZulu-Natal, 2011, p. 28, 32.

33 Ibid., p. 34.

34 D. Gengan, "The Msunduzi Municipality, City of Pietermaritzburg" Presentation to WIEGO Colloquium on World Class Cities and the Urban Informal Economy: Inclusive Planning for the Working Poor, 2006.

35 Ibid., p. 40.

36 Robbins and Hobbs, "Cities with Jobs" p. 39.

37 Ibid.

38 J. Coates, A. Swindale and P. Bilinsky, "Household Food Insecurity Access Scale (HFIAS) for Measurement of Food Access: Indicator Guide (Version 3)" Food and Nutrition Technical Assistance Project, Academy for Educational Development, Washington, D.C., 2007.

39 A. Swindale and P. Bilinsky, "Household Dietary Diversity Score (HDDS) for Measurement of Household Food Access: Indicator Guide (Version 2)" Food and Nutrition Technical Assistance Project, Academy for Educational Development, Washington, D.C., 2006.

40 P. Bilinsky and A. Swindale, "Months of Adequate Household Food Provisioning (MAHFP) for Measurement of Household Food Access: Indicator Guide" Food and Nutrition Technical Assistance Project, Academy for Educational Development, Washington, D.C., 2007.

41 "Urban Agriculture in Msunduzi Municipality, South Africa" *RUAF Magazine* December 2007, pp. 39-41.

42 B. Njokwe and J. McCosh, "African Roots Project" Workshop on Urban Micro-Farming and HIV-AIDS, Johannesburg/Cape Town, 2005, p.4.

43 G. Hampwaye, E. Nel and C. Rogerson, "Urban Agriculture as Local Initiative in Lusaka, Zambia" *Environment and Planning C: Government and Policy* 25(4) (2007): 553-72; D. Simatele and T. Binns, "Motivation and Marginalization in African Urban Agriculture: The Case of Lusaka, Zambia" *Urban Forum* 19(1) (2008): 1-21; C. Mutonodzo, "The Social and Economic Implications of Urban Agriculture on Food Security in Harare, Zimbabwe" In M. Redwood, ed., *Agriculture in Urban Planning: Generating Livelihoods and Food Security* (London and Ottawa: Earthscan and IDRC, 2009), pp. 73-89.

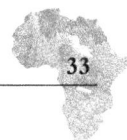

44   B. Frayne, "Pathways of Food: Mobility and Food Transfers in Southern African Cities" *International Development Planning Review* 32(2010): 291–310.

45   See, for example, E. Alvi and S. Dendir, "Private Transfers, Informal Loans and Risk Sharing Among Poor Urban Households in Ethiopia" *Journal of Development Studies* 45(2009): 1325-43.

46   J. Crush and B. Frayne, "Supermarket Expansion and the Informal Food Economy in Southern African Cities: Implications for Urban Food Security" *Journal of Southern African Studies* 37(2011): 781–807.

47   H. Madevu, "Competition in the Tridimensional Urban Fresh Produce Retail Market: The Case of the Tshwane Metropolitan Area, South Africa" MSc Thesis, University of Pretoria, 2006.

48   S. Naidoo, S. Govender and J. Green, "The Role of Supermarkets in Local Government and Environmental and Socio-Economic Sustainability" MIDI Report, Msunduzi, 2010. Our thanks to Paul Crankshaw for sharing a copy of this report and for information and discussion of its aims and objectives.

49   Mkondeni is a fresh produce market (similar to those in other major South African cities) owned by the Municipality and operated by buying agents who purchase in bulk from commercial farmers, sell on to a range of formal and informal sector customers and pay a fixed percentage of their takings to the Municipality; see A. Rylance, "Enhancing the Prospects of Small Scale and Informal Retailers in Fresh Produce Value Chains: An Examination of the Developmental Impact of Public Sector Market Facilities on Formal and Informal Retailers in Selected KwaZulu-Natal Markets" MA Thesis, University of KwaZulu-Natal, 2008.

50   L. Steyn, "Stores Score on Pension Payday" *Mail & Guardian* 3 February 2012.

51   Rylance, "Small Scale and Informal Retailers in Fresh Produce Chains" pp. 41, 57.

52   Naidoo et al, "Role of Supermarkets."

53   K. Joynt, "How Have the Poor Responded to the Increase in the Price of Food? A Case Study of Pimville, Soweto" M.A. Thesis, University of Witwatersrand, 2008; M. Cohen and J. Garett, "The Food Price Crisis and Urban Food (In) security" *Environment and Urbanization* 22 (2010): 467-82; P. Jacobs, "Protecting Food Insecure Households Against Rapid Food Price Inflation" HSRC Policy Brief, Pretoria, 2012.

54   J. Battersby, "Beyond the Food Desert: Finding Ways to Speak about Urban Food Security in South Africa" *Geografiska Annaler: Series B* 94 (2012): 141–59.

55   Msunduzi Municipality, *Integrated Development Plan 2011-2016 and Beyond*, p. 5.

56   B. Dodson, A. Chiweza and L. Riley, *Gender and Food Insecurity in Southern African Cities*, AFSUN Urban Food Security Series No 10, Cape Town, 2012.

57   D. Warshawsky, *Urban Food Insecurity and the Advent of Food Banking in Southern Africa*, AFSUN Urban Food Security Series No. 6, Cape Town, 2011.

www.ingramcontent.com/pod-product-compliance
Lightning Source LLC
Chambersburg PA
CBHW080135270326
41926CB00021B/4493